AF211943

NATE INSLEE

REAL LIFE ORGANIZING

The Necessary Guide to Get Your Life In Order, Learn Useful Methods and Tips On How You Can Get More Organized In Life

Descrierea CIP a Bibliotecii Naţionale a României
NATE INSLEE
   REAL LIFE ORGANIZING. The Ultimate Guide To Artificial
Intelligence in Digital Marketing, Discover The Ways on How You
Can Use Artificial Intelligence to Help Your Business Grow and
Succeed / Nate Inslee. – Bucharest: Editura My Ebook, 2020
   ISBN

NATE INSLEE

REAL LIFE ORGANIZING

The Necessary Guide to Get Your Life In Order, Learn Useful Methods and Tips On How You Can Get More Organized In Life

My Ebook Publishing House
Bucharest, 2020

TABLE OF CONTENTS

CHAPTER 1

THE BASICS ON ORGANIZATION

Synopsis

Every person comes with a New Year's resolution and one of these is about the ability to make things in order. Every person believes that if he or she will be organized in everything, he or she will become a better person.

Yes, that is correct but getting started with it will let a person face difficulties and challenges as he or she takes the journey towards becoming efficient when it comes to organization.

However, getting what you wanted will never be impossible if you know the basics. The following are the 4 primary organizing principles that could help you in regaining authority over your environment, your everyday schedule and of course, your life.

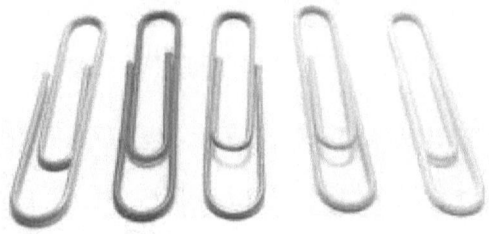

The Basics

Clearing Out the Mess

People suffer from the so-called "overload" which means too much obligations, excessive stuffs, too much details and many more. Clearing out the mess indicates that you have to get rid of anything which is not important to your life. Keep in mind that untidiness takes up time, energy, space and even your money without giving you any advantage. You will find clutter in various aspects of your life such as in relationships wherein some people are not giving support to your goals and they try to pull you down.

It also comes with finances involving inefficient spending patterns and in the physical space wherein you have some possessions that you don't use. Clutter can also be found in schedule wherein there are interruptions that hold you back and it can also affect your emotions as you experience guilt, jealousy or you have unrealistic expectations. You have to create a plan on how you will clear them out one by one.

Allot a Space for All

Did you know the reason behind the physical clutter? Well, that is you don't look for a place where you can put your stuffs. When you are already finished in using them, you have to keep them back to where they should be. Hence, you should provide a place where they must be stored. Why don't you use neat containers and label them? The use of these materials will be the most ideal way to ensure that all materials you use are organized and kept properly. Likewise, you should keep in mind the following:

- You have to store the items in the space that is nearest to where you use them
- Make sure that all of them are grouped together
- Keep climatic issues in mind
- Make all regularly used items more handy

Develop a System

You can manage your everyday activities in 2 ways. First, you can perform them randomly which means you need to decide about the way you should do those tasks. The second option is you do them systematically which means you do not necessarily need to put more effort on thinking how you have to do your tasks. Your effort as well as your time should be focused on finishing the activities and you must able to complete them faster.

Assess and Change Your Systems

System setup is such a brilliant step to take in becoming well organized. If you employ the system that you use for years, you may not be able to meet your needs in the same way you used to. Hence, you have to assess your systems to find out if still they can help you or not. If there are problems, better to change them with the new ones.

Getting better organized could be a daunting task but with the help of these principles, you will never fail in meeting your goal. What you need is to take some simple steps so that all aspects of your life will be in order.

CHAPTER 2

IDENTIFY WHERE YOUR ORGANIZATION HAS ISSUES

Synopsis

Maybe you are now trying to learn how to become an organized individual. You have the system to follow and you know the dos and don'ts but still, you don't get what you desire. If you experience this kind of scenario, you have to reevaluate everything to see where your organization problems are. To meet success, you should be able to identify the areas of your life where there are unresolved issues.

Where Are The Issues

As said before, you will find clutter in different life aspects. To find out the concealed problems that pull you down, you should check these aspects one by one. First, you must focus your attention to your relationships with the people who surround you. There are people who are always there for you and they really show their support to your decisions and desires in life.

On the other way around, you will also find others who are against you; they are the ones who are not interested to your aims in life. They don't want to support you and the worst thing is that they don't like to see you happy and successful. What they do is pulling you down and they will try every possible way just to get what they want for you.

You must observe and take time to think in order to find out if this area of your life stops you from achieving access. Then, do something you think that will be helpful to overcome the problem.

If you think that your relationship with everybody is okay, then you should proceed to finances. When it comes to this aspect of life, the problem here could be you practice wasteful spending. Again, only you will be the one who can identify if the problem is about your finances.

You have to be a practical buyer; you need to be wise when it comes to spending your money. Before you buy something, think first of it; it must be something useful to your life. It should be something that you don't have. If not, you will just waste your money for that. To become organized, you'll have to avoid careless spending patterns.

Also, your problem can be physically. Perhaps, you keep some materials which you don't use anymore. You have to get rid of them and there are best ways on how you can get rid of your unwanted possessions. One of these is to give them as donations and another one is to sell them. Those things that can be used by somebody else are the ones you have to sell or donate.

In organizing your possessions, you have to find a good place where you can store them. Arrange and group them; by doing this, you will find those stuffs which are not important to you anymore. Check them and see to it that they are still in good condition if you plan to donate or sell them.

Also, you might become unorganized if there are interruptions in your everyday schedule. To avoid this, you should create a schedule for all tasks you have to accomplish. Also, try to focus your attention to a specific task first before you proceed to the other. If something stops you from doing it then thinking of a way on how you can finish your obligation although interruptions came in should be done.

All of these aspects require your time and attention. Failure to check them one by one will stop you from meeting success in your attempt to become more organized for the coming year.

CHAPTER 3

HOW ORGANIZATION AFFECTS YOUR LIFE

Synopsis

Every person desires to practice a well-organized routine throughout his or her life. It is primarily because he or she knows the possible benefits that he or she can get from doing it. You should know that organization can greatly affect your life and it can lead you to such good things. If you practice organization then you will see that all things around you fall into place. You will be more able to avoid rushing as you forgot to bring something when going out. Likewise, you will feel more relaxed as well as less stressful every day.

The Impact

Practicing organization would provide more time for you to perform other things that you like to do. You know where you should go in getting something you need and wasting time in searching for tiny things that have been misplaced will be reduced. When you are an organized person, you would see your relatives and loved ones more often without rushing off again as you failed to perform a particular task.

Lack of organization could leave you anxious and stressed from time to time. It will make you feel uncomfortable when someone decides to go to your home unexpectedly. You will surely feel this kind of emotion most especially if all of the parts of your home are messy. This will make you unhappy and embarrassed as your visitor sees the condition of your home.

If you are an organized individual, you become happier and healthier. You will be able to have spare time that you can use to visit the gym or you can prepare and cook more foods for your loved ones. Likewise, your professional life will be enhanced when you practice organization.

Otherwise, you will find yourself spending more time for a specific obligation that you can supposedly finish in just a few minutes.

Another benefit that you can get from becoming an organized person is that you can save money. When you make all things you use arranged well, you will be able to avoid spending your money for a particular product only to discover after few days that there's one kept inside your messy cabinet. If you practice good organization, achieving more good things in life will never be hard for you to do. Keep in mind that being unorganized will just lead you to a miserable life.

CHAPTER 4

WHAT MAKES GOOD ORGANIZATION

Synopsis

There are several questions that may come inside of your mind when it talks about organization. One of these is the question "what makes good organization". Well, it has something to do with the qualities that you should possess to become an organized individual. These abilities will lead you towards practicing good organization.

Good Organization

8 Abilities of Organized Individuals

1. They consider things before they take steps. They make sure that they always do the right thing. They think of it and they imagine how they will be able to finish it while they figure out

the right time for taking the necessary steps to accomplish that specific task.

2. They are good planners. Those people who practice good organization are fond of making a list for everything they intend to perform. They also do the same thing about the way they should finish their tasks.

3. They use a calendar. Organized persons make use of a calendar so that they will never forget the succeeding appointments they have.

4. They choose the jobs they have to prioritize. Those people who practice good organization are aware that the most valuable tasks they have are those in which they have to focus their attention first. It helps them in avoiding stress knowing that they can always meet the deadlines at all times.

5. They hate clutter. Good organization requires people to get rid of mess like listing too many things to be remembered.

6. They take breaks. Those people who follow good organization don't make a schedule of "fun times". They always have the spare time to relax and enjoy.

7. Their life remains simple. Getting rid of the things that may control their lives and going back to the ordinary portion of life are few of the things that organized people do. If they have too much meetings to attend for a day, they try to negotiate for

some of these to be rescheduled. If they have lots of chores to be done, they look for the most convenient way to get them finished.

8. They come up with a routine which becomes a practice. For organized individuals, a routine is like a guide and they can change it to make this suitable for them if the need for modification arises.

All of these things will help you in becoming a better and organized one. If you lack good organization in your life then you must consider these things and reap the benefits that only proper organization can give.

CHAPTER 5

WHAT MAKES BAD ORGANIZATION

Synopsis

Now that you have learned what makes good organization, it's the right time for you to learn something about bad organization. Did you know the qualities that unorganized persons have? Keep in mind that being unorganized will not bring any benefit to your life so you have to change yourself.

Being unorganized might be considered as a disorder which is typically called chronically disorganized. This can excessively affect your whole life especially if you failed to seek guidance. You will never be able to get rid of it overtime but ignoring the problem will just make the situation worse.

Just like you, people who suffer from it generally come with a history of ineffectiveness and they tend to weaken the quality of their lives. To overcome this, these persons should seek assistance for a specific period of time and probably on a constant basis.

Unorganized individuals possess the following characteristics:

- Persons who practice bad organization are actually the ones who are very intelligent. Typically, they are blessed with special abilities. They can be somewhat complicated to distinguish because these persons are exceptional when it comes to hiding their problems. Chronic disorganization typically emerges later in their lives while they become more complicated and demanding. That is the time that you can recognize people who are unorganized individuals.

- Individuals who are not organized are those who are creative and they possess a highly creative personality. They show interest in everything that results to attention loss. They also fail to spend time wisely and they are searching for better strategies that can lead to continuous changes. Unorganized persons also fail to follow the plans which they have prepared. Routines and orderliness become dull or uninteresting in their lives.

- Individuals who practice bad organization are the ones who are typically dominated by their brains' right side. These people can be a dreamer, an artist or a musician. These individuals like to maintain materials exposed that can end to out of vision view of thoughts. It leads right-brained individuals to bad organization.

- Persons who are chronically disorganized are more likely to possess changeable interests. It is hard for them to stick with one task to do as these people tend to get jaded easily. Hence, they proceed to another task for psychological stimulation and enthusiasm. This kind of attitude results to lack of dedication to schedule, structure as well as to organization.

- Those who practice bad organization tend to have an unhealthy emotional connection to stuffs. They usually give utmost value to some materials as these persons become excessively emotionally attached to stuffs. This character leads to the incapability to discard those items although they are not useful anymore making it hard for them to get organized.

These qualities are all of those things that build bad organization. To meet what you wanted in life, you must change these characteristics if you have one.

CHAPTER 6

TOOLS FOR BETTER ORGANIZATION

Synopsis

As you wish to become a well-prepared and an organized person in the coming year, you must be aware of the tools that you can use to achieve positive results in the end. It is considered to be the last quest for someone who tries to be more organized and productive. Since the most suitable organization tool for you might be not be the same with what your friend should use, the following tools will always be the best for almost everyone. The selection of the tools that you must use will always depend on your needs.

Tools

- Google calendar – this tool will let you keep your whole life organized intuitively and without slow interface or inconveniences.

- Backpack – it is always ideal for your to-do lists as well as in other forms of lists that you have.

- A pile of 3 x 5 sized index cards – these can be an omnipresent capture tool for you. With these cards, you can keep your to-do lists that are context-based, your notes as well as your project list. These tools are very modifiable, handy and convenient to use.

- Landing strip close to the front door – it can be used for unloading all your stuffs so everything stays organized. Likewise, you will not forget anything you have to bring when you go out. You can have it in any style you prefer. However, a reader's setup is composed of a group of hooks designed for backpacks and lunch kits. You can have a box that holds your keys, mobile phone, your sunglasses and other materials you have.

- The rubbish can – you have to separate your unimportant stuffs from those that you use. It is very important to reduce before you start organizing your possessions. Put inside the trash can all items that are not absolutely important to you at all.

- Stick notes on the desktop – you may use sticky notes in which you will write all of your tasks for the day. These will serve as your guide in your attempt to complete all your tasks within that day. Once you completed one of the tasks successfully, mark it with your ballpen.

- A list of your habit – aside from having your to-do lists, you also need to make a list of your habit. This will keep the action list you use from becoming plagued by your daily tasks.

Also, there are some apps that you can also use so that you will become more successful in your attempt to become organized. All you need is to do some research to find these apps through the web.

CHAPTER 7

THE BENEFITS OF ORGANIZATION

Synopsis

Knowing how to be organized will bring different benefits to your life. With your effort and determination to succeed, you will be able to reap such advantages. Always keep in mind that organization is the key to become successful in life so you really need to be highly motivated in learning how to become efficient in organizing your possessions and your whole life.

The Benefits of Organization

You Become Great

One of the major advantages that you can get from practicing proper organization is how this will make you look. When somebody goes to your home, he or she will be impressed by the way you arrange your personal belongings and in the cleanliness of your house. Keeping your home organized and clean at all times is typically a complicated task.

In order for you to meet this objective, you have to be dependable. You should never stop from cleaning the house and hope that it will stay organized for a very long time.

Always return all your stuffs on the place where they should be and you must be flexible and willing to modify your system whenever you have to make changes to it. Also, you have to use the materials that will help you a lot in organizing all your stuffs. All of these will help you in making your home as a better place to live.

You Stay Worry-Free

Also, being an organized person will set you free from all of your worries. Organizing everything especially the things that you use in your everyday life will let you find them easily. You will be able to avoid experiencing panic because you are already late for work or school but still you can't go as you have to look for a particular item that you have to bring. Being organized in life will also be less stressful since everything is okay. You will always be relaxed and you feel comfortable at all times.

You Avoid Wasting Your Money

You will also be more able to save money. It will be easier for you to prevent wasteful spending like buying a new pad of paper because you can no longer find the one that you have purchased last month.

All of these are the benefits that you can enjoy when you become a well- organized person. If you want to live with utmost comfort and persistent success throughout your life, you have to stand up, take the necessary steps and be determined in changing yourself by practicing organization.

CHAPTER 8

STAYING MOTIVATED FOR MAINTAINING ORGANIZATION

Synopsis

Motivation is also important for you to able to maintain organization. It is said that organizing is like a journey. You were able to reach your goal and reap the benefits that it can provide but still it's not the end. Organizing is a continuous journey as opposite to the one-time deal. For sure, you experience success in every step of the way. You notice that everything is okay including your home, your schedule and your life. It makes you happy and satisfied.

Motivation

However, things may go back in the way they used to. You will use again the items that you have arranged yesterday, you have new tasks to do and you went out to buy new items which you have to store somewhere. Life continues and during the process, the clutter may also come in. This is not the point of being organized. The ultimate aim for turning yourself into an organized individual is not actually to get into the destination called "organization" and remain there for a lifetime. Instead, your goal is that you should be able to reach that destination so that you can pass over it and move to somewhere else. That is the place wherein you live while you enjoy your life.

If you have been discouraged to continue as you have to perform again the task that you have completed few hours ago, then you may tell yourself that it is really hard to accept that organizing is a continuous journey. How will you be able to stay motivated and determined to take this never-ending job? Well, here are some tips for you to follow:

- Shift your viewpoint – you have to embrace everyday clutter because it is an indication that you are living a productive, full and cheerful life.

- Tidy up often – instead of being destructed by everyday clutter which is the result of living your own life, choose to clean and place the things back to where they must be regularly. Why don't you look for empty containers or boxes to use as carriers of your valuables and look for the best areas where you must put them? This way, arranging all your stuff will be more enjoyable and hassle-free for you to do every day.

- Do regular evaluation of your stuffs – reassess all your belongings frequently. Keep in mind that the lesser items you keep, the lesser time you will spend in dealing with them. When your house is filled with only those stuffs that you use daily, you will spend more time in living as well as in having fun with your life.

- Be cautious and keep your goal in mind – to keep all aspects of your life in an organized way, you should keep them clutter-free. Be careful in taking each step of your organization system to avoid problems. Remember the benefits that organization can provide to your life in order to keep yourself motivated throughout the journey.

- Keep your organization system simple – when it comes to organization, you will be in need of a particular system to use.

Always remember that it must be simple so that organizing everything will be less difficult to accomplish.

- Keep on using the organizing solutions that you love – when you appreciate the solution you employ then you will have fun in using it. To stay motivated in organizing, you must figure out the outcome of every step that you will take. Go for the organizing solutions that are efficient enough in helping you maintain your motivation.

CHAPTER 9

STAYING ON TRACK

Synopsis

Do you wish to know that you are doing good as you do your best to become efficient in organizing? Well, to find out if you are on the right track, you need to monitor your progress. Staying on the right track involves determining where you are today and where you would like to go. Follow these helpful tips to get started:

How to Stay on Track to Get Organized Successfully

1. Before you do anything, you must see to it that you are about to take the right step. Think about your system and be dedicated to follow each step that it dictates to you so that you will never lose yourway.

2. In order to become a person who is efficient in organizing, you have to possess some important qualities. You are on your way to success once you are able to develop them. These traits are the following:

- Focus and determination to reach the goal

- A positive behavior or being optimistic

- Patience and the power to endure difficulties

- The ability to overcome destructions

- Ability to manage time

- The capability to solve problems and interruptions that may hold you back

- Compliance to follow the organizing system you chose

3. Also, you have to think about the possible problems that you may encounter throughout your journey. You should deal with them and that is by preparing effective solutions that you can use to solve them. Don't let them drag you down or else you will fail to stay on track.

4. Include in the content of the checklist all of the goals that you would like to achieve.

5. You need to look at your checklist and assess yourself from time to time. It is important to evaluate your current knowledge as well as your attitude. Since you have learned the

qualities of an unorganized individual, you have to do your part and change your behavior especially if you have any of the negative traits that have been discussed previously. You should include all good qualities that you must develop in the content of your checklist. These qualities are those that make good organization and you should replace the bad ones with these. Focus your attention right from the start of your journey to this idea. By using your checklist, you have to put a check to the qualities you have acquired then leave unmarked what you don't have yet.

6. If you notice that something wrong comes along your way, go back to your checklist. This is to avoid losing all your efforts that you have exerted since from the beginning.

7. Don't forget that everything you do is for your own sake. Remember the advantages that you can get from being good when it comes to organizing. Take these benefits as your motivator in order to bear confidence and full determination to attain your goal.

Staying on track might be the most challenging part of this very crucial journey. Yet, if you are really eager to succeed then all of the challenges that you may encounter anytime will never get the chance to defeat you.

CHAPTER 10

MAKING RESOLUTIONS FOR ORGANIZATION

The present year is about to end and just like other people; you want to make yourself better for the next one. If you want to be a more organized individual for the coming year then you should start making organizing resolutions that will stick. The start of another year is also the best time for renewing or making a dedication to get all things in order.

However, promising to be organized could be overwhelming and unattainable just like the other forms of resolutions for New Year. This time, you better set aside your guilt and fear of disappointment then think of organizing resolutions which will stick. Please consider the following steps:

Concentrate on Your Reason First

What encourages you to learn how to be good in terms of organizing? Every person who aims for this may come up with various reasons. For instance, it can be disappointment because of spending more time every day in searching for all stuffs you require or you lose more of your money because you pay penalties for your overdue utility bills.

Regardless of the reasons you have, just keep them within your mind starting today and in the coming days, weeks and months. Making a sticky note about them is also a good idea. You can attach this note on the door of your refrigerator, on your desk or to where you can see them every day.

Make Realistic Resolutions

Complex resolutions seem to be encouraging in the first glance but sticking to them could be very difficult. However, quick resolutions will just lead you to failure and embarrassment. This time, you have to choose resolutions that are attainable and realistic.

For instance, instead of swearing to revamp the organization of your home, prefer a specific room or section of it like the kitchen or the façade hall closet. After that, you must break your objective into small portions such as how to get rid of the unnecessary materials you have and organizing those which you have to keep so that you can easily find them whenever you require them. You have to do some easy maintenance tasks for each week. This way, you can keep up your progress.

When you attained one of your resolutions successfully and you are willing to make others then you are doing good. If you don't, just remind yourself about your goals then recommit to your promise.

Aim for the Change that Will Last Longer

Lastly, bear in your mind that it is better to go for changes that will last longer than those which may happen instantly but may last only for a while. Be aware that slow and steady development will lead you to a long lasting change. At first, you may not be happy with this but your patience will be paid in the long run.

So now, you may start planning how to prepare yourself for a change and that's all about organization. Remember what you have learned here and bear undying strength of mind to obtain your goal in the end. Wish you all the best!

Printed by Libri Plureos GmbH in Hamburg,
Germany